The Local Historian at Work 6
General Editor: Alan Crosby

TITHES

Maps, Apportionments and the 1836 Act

PROFESSOR ERIC J. EVANS, MA, PhD
Department of History,
Lancaster University

Published by PHILLIMORE for
BRITISH ASSOCIATION FOR LOCAL HISTORY

First published 1978

Revised edition

1993

Published for
BRITISH ASSOCIATION FOR LOCAL HISTORY
by PHILLIMORE & CO. LTD.
Shopwyke Manor Barn, Chichester, Sussex

ISBN 0 85033 857 3

Printed and bound by St Richard's Press, Chichester.

CONTENTS

ILLUSTRATIONS

Plates i, iii and iv, and the cover illustration, are reproduced by kind permission of the County Archivist of Lancashire: plates i, iii and iv are from the Marton Tithe Apportionment, D.R.B. 1/130.

INTRODUCTION TO THE FIRST EDITION

The Tithe Commutation Act of 1836 is something of a forgotten landmark in English agrarian and social history. It has received less attention than it deserves,[1] for it settled a major irritant in rural society and enabled agricultural investment to be planned on a more rational basis. John Wilson Croker, a regular contributor to Tory journals in the 1820s and 1830s, acknowledged in 1836 that the Commutation Act had been 'the most important passed in the session' but had 'excited comparatively little observation'. He explained that 'it was an English Bill of deep and real importance, and the English gentry, even the few radicals who may be reckoned in that class would not permit great and permanent interests to be made the plaything of faction – a tub to be tossed and lashed about by the tail of the leviathan'.[2] By the 1830s both major parties acknowledged the need to remove the iniquities and the irritations of the old tithe system. The Church of England, fearing for its very establishment status against radical attacks, acquiesced in parliamentary interference with its property – a reaction which would have been inconceivable even ten years earlier. In addition, the Act was a complex statute, dealing not only with broad principles but with minute technicalities of property right. Important though it was, it neither stirred the blood nor afforded partisans easy points to score off each other in heated debate. Its very impenetrability eased its passage.

By the Tithe Commutation Act traditional tithes – based on a tenth of the produce of and nourished by the earth – were converted into rent charge payments based on the prevailing price of grain.

INTRODUCTION TO THE SECOND EDITION

It is hoped that, during the past fifteen years, *Tithes and the Tithe Commutation Act, 1836* (the title of the first edition) has met its main purpose of informing readers about a previously understudied aspect of agricultural history and about a statute which had been little studied but which was of great importance to nineteenth-century landowners and farmers.

A second edition should not seek to rewrite the first. The broad conclusions reached in 1978 still stand. The Tithe Commutation Act, minor irritations about its specific provisions apart, was an enormous boon both to farmers and to tithe owners. It replaced vexation and contention with certainty and an important degree of rationality. It also played a far from insignificant part in helping to stabilize the economic position of the Church of England and in shoring up its social position. Calls for Disestablishment – loud and strident in the early 1830s – were far less frequently heard by the third quarter of the nineteenth century.

It is not necessary here, therefore, fundamentally to reappraise what was written in the first edition. However, some valuable work has been done since 1978 and it is important that those wishing to learn more about tithes, or wanting to make use of the mass of source material which the Tithe Commutation Act engendered after 1836, should be aware of it. This Introduction offers a brief guide to recent research.

One substantial book on the Church of England in the period of Commutation appeared in the 1980s. Peter Virgin, *The Church in an Age of Negligence: Ecclesiastical Structure and Problems of Church Reform 1700-1840* (James Clarke, Cambridge, 1989) discusses the Tithe Commutation Act, but its assessment of the importance of the statute reflects earlier work and does not revise its conclusions. Of more significance to tithe studies are Roger Kain and Hugh Prince: *The Tithe Surveys of England and Wales* (Cambridge University Press, 1985) and Roger Kain, *An Atlas and Index of the Tithe Files of Mid-Nineteenth Century England and Wales* (Cambridge University Press, 1986). Both volumes are rooted in substantial research. The volume by Kain and Prince includes chapters on the Tithe Commutation Act, Tithe maps, apportionments and files and on the accuracy of the surveys themselves. The evidence provided by the tithe files, now housed in the

Public Record Office at Kew, is discussed in detail. The authors' conclusion, that the tithe surveys contain an enormous volume of 'apposite, synchronic data ... from which patterns of land use, crops, fields, farms and estates can be reconstructed' (p.256), is evidently true, and they are also entirely correct to enter the important caveat that 'the surveys contain relatively little information on the processes of agrarian change'.

Roger Kain's *Atlas* is an invaluable work of reference. It provides a county by county survey of the process of commutation. The reader can use it to derive information about land use in each of the 14,829 tithe districts of England and Wales. The statistical place index refers the reader to each tithe district, using the reference numbers adopted by the PRO. Thanks to Kain's work, students of tithe now have a complete digest of that part of the work of the tithe commission which survived the weeding process. The index is particularly valuable in providing information about the type of evidence – such as rotation practices, quality of pasture, and new crops – available for each District. All students, both of land use in the first half of the nineteenth century and of the diversity of tithing practice at the time of commutation, should make use of Kain's *Atlas* after gaining a general introduction to the subject from the introductory material which follows.

Volume 6 of the Cambridge *Agrarian History of England and Wales*, edited by Gordon Mingay, covers the period 1750-1850 and was published in 1989. It is, of course, an indispensable work of reference, though it could be objected that treatment of tithes is less extensive than might have been expected. The present author has provided a specific chapter on tithes in the seventeenth century and early eighteenth centuries in the *Agrarian History* vol. 5, part 2 (Cambridge, 1985), pp.389-405.

The implications of using a seven-year average of prices as the basis for tithe commutation has been specifically studied by Wray Vamplew in 'Tithes and Agriculture: Some Comments on Commutation', *Economic History Review* 2nd series xxxiv, no. 1 (1981), pp.115-119. He concludes, somewhat differently from me, that 'the use of corn averages [in] ... the mechanism of tithe commutation ... had little consequence for tithe payments, although farmers in a few areas would be advantaged or disadvantaged where local septennial prices exhibited different fluctuations from the official ones'. The important factor was the septennial price itself since, although this was a stabilizing factor, it could result 'in farmers increasing or reducing [tithe] payments at times when farm incomes may have been doing the opposite' (p.119). Vamplex agrees with me that the most important element in the commutation process was that tithe no longer operated as a tax on yield. Farmers in the later nineteenth century could benefit from switching from grain into livestock production. If they did so they 'were able to reduce tithe payments as a proportion of their income from agriculture'. Readers wishing to follow this aspect of nineteenth-century agricultural history should also consult W. Vamplew, 'A Grain of Truth: The Nineteenth Century Corn Averages', *Agricultural History Review, xxxiii* (1980), pp.1-17.

Other work of relevance published in the last decade includes G. M. Ditchfield, 'Parliament, the Quakers and the Tithe Question, 1750-1835', *Parliamentary History* iv (1985), pp. 87-114; Maurice J. Bric, 'The Tithe System in Eighteenth-Century Ireland', *Proceedings of the Royal Irish Academy* Section C lxxxvi (1986), 7, pp.271-88 and – an extremely valuable insight into land use from another important primary source – A. D. M. Phillips, 'Agricultural Land Use and Cropping in Cheshire around 1880: Some Evidence from Cropping Books', *Transactions of the Lancashire and Cheshire Antiquarian Society* lxxxiv (1987), pp.46-63. Paul Hindle discusses tithe maps in *Maps for Local History* (Batsford, 1988), pp.56-60.

The overall reflection on nineteenth-century tithe studies since the appearance of the first edition of this study would be that, although the basic conclusions about the importance of the tithe question have not been seriously challenged, far more evidence is now available in reference form for the student to use. Tithe studies, both for themselves and as an adjunct to local history research, are more accessible than ever before.

EDITOR'S FOREWORD

The first edition of this book was produced by the erstwhile Standing Conference for Local History, as part of its series 'National Statutes and the Local Community'. The volumes in this series described the situation prior to the enactment of those Acts of Parliament, the manner in which the Acts were enforced, their implications for local communities at the time, and the documentary evidence which is available to local historians today.

The original series was jointly edited by Jenny Kermode and the late Joe Bagley, both of the University of Liverpool. The exercise of their editorial role called for knowledge and understanding, and a willingness to contribute – in whatever measure might be required – from their resources of time and energy. Gratitude is expressed to them for their work.

Since 1978, when the book was first published, interest in and enthusiasm for local history have developed at an unprecedented rate. There are many more local history societies, many more local history publications, and many more individuals who are actively researching and recording the history of their localities. The Standing Conference has metamorphosed into the British Association for Local History, which has a fast-growing membership and an extensive range of activities and publications.

The first edition was immediately recognised as the best basic introduction to a complex and difficult subject, and it soon sold out. The publication of this revised edition will therefore be widely welcomed. I would like to thank Professor Eric Evans for allowing us to republish the book and for his work on revisions and a new Introduction, undertaken despite a very heavy workload.

ALAN CROSBY
General Editor, B. A. L. H.

Chapter I

TITHE COLLECTION BEFORE 1836

Originally tithes were payable only in kind. The incumbent of a parish made tithing tours to collect the tenth sheaf of corn, the tenth pig, sheep or cow, and even the tenth pail of milk, when the farmer signified that the produce was ready. The difficulties of collecting tithes in this way, even in a compact and flat parish, were considerable. In large, mountainous parishes, remote from the markets where produce could be sold, they were insuperable. But not all the difficulties were encountered by the tithe owner. By custom in many places the farmer could not remove his hay or corn crop from the field until the tithe owner or his appointed agent had taken his tithe. The purpose was obviously to avoid fraud; but if the tithe owner delayed his appearance and the weather was foul in the meantime, the crop might be severely damaged. Even where the farmer removed his nine-tenths, the tithe owner's non-appearance would prevent the farmer from re-ploughing his land or setting it to pasture until collection was made.

In most English parishes the glebe terrier set out in some detail the custom to be followed in collecting tithes. In general, customs were precise and restrictive; they invited, and frequently got, reprisals.[3] Canny farmers were usually more than a match for callow incumbents who, coming to a new parish, tried to establish the tithe rights their terriers allowed them. A year or two's vexation and frustration persuaded many to accept money compositions in lieu of tithe. These money compositions, obvious victims of future inflation, were originally set well below the nominal value of the tithe if collected in kind. Commonly, tithe owners agreed with farmers to take so much per acre in lieu of tithe. Payments fluctuated greatly, but at the end of the eighteenth century, wheat at 7s-8s., oats and barley at 4s-5s. and meadow and pasture land at 1s 6d. to 3s. were common.[4] Aristocratic impropriators and other influential tithe owners might commission yearly valuations and threaten defaulters with legal action if their assessments were not met; but even they did not always achieve success. The Duke of Sutherland, one of the richest men in Britain, had enormous trouble collecting tithes from recalcitrant farmers in Codsall (Staffs.). Between 1829 and 1849, arrears of payments mounted steadily until they totalled the equivalent of one-and-a-half years' payment.[5] The Sutherland agent thought it more prudent to carry these losses rather than risk the still greater odium of litigation.

Compositions invariably resulted in reduced tithe yield. The Rev. John Thirkens wrote in 1828 to Thomas Green, M.P. for Lancaster and an ardent tithe reformer, explaining: 'I do really think I don't get much more than a fourth part of my dues – if I collected the tithes in kind the land occupiers would harass me to death.'[6] William Jones, vicar of Broxbourne and Hoddesdon (Herts.), was 'confident that I am defrauded by many of my parishioners of various vicarial dues and rights to which the laws of heaven and earth entitle me'.[7] When assistant tithe commissioners implemented the details of the Tithe Commutation Act in the later 1830s and 1840s they regularly deducted between 20 and 40 per cent of the nominal value as collection expenses.[8] But, because compositions usually avoided bickering and strife, most tithes had been unofficially commuted to money payments before the end of the eighteenth century. These compositions, however, could revert to payment in kind at the behest of the tithe owner if he wished to reassert his rights – for example, at the beginning of incumbency or when tithe disputes arose. The extent to which tithing in kind survived should not be underestimated. Lord Ernle, largely on the evidence of the Board of Agriculture county reviewers, stated that in-kind payments survived only in the extreme north-west, parts of the south – particularly

Hampshire and Kent – and in Cambridgeshire and Suffolk.[9] Evidence collected by F. M. Eden, in his pioneering study of the English poor, and for William Pitt when he contemplated tithe commutation in 1791-2, showed that in-kind payments were common in Bedfordshire, Lancashire, Lincolnshire and Shropshire, as well as in the areas indicated by Ernle.[10] In-kind payments were normally restricted to the more valuable crops such as oats and barley, and especially wheat.

Those who insisted on tithing in kind courted hostility. A very large number of tithe owners, nevertheless, were prepared to brave the odium which inevitably followed a sustained attempt to improve tithe revenues. After all, the stakes were large. A successful action which established, for example, the right to the full tithe of a crop from which previously only small customary payments, or 'moduses', had been made, could treble or even quadruple the tithe owner's income. A 'modus' was a traditional and unvaried payment, deemed to represent the equivalent to a full tithe at a time before the limit of legal memory (1189). It had received the sanctity of custom by long usage and would be upheld by the courts as a valid payment in lieu of tithe if evidence to the effect that it had indeed been received by the tithe owner consistently and over a long period were produced. By the end of the eighteenth century, therefore, modus values were derisorily low.

Impropriators, and more particularly the tithe-farmers who held leases from them, were naturally tempted to try their luck if they had to contend with moduses; and incumbents could plausibly argue that, since they were life-tenants not owners, any derogation of their duty in pursuing tithe claims would rebound to the detriment of their successors. Above all, tithe law and custom was so complex that disputes gave rise to endless legal wrangles, from which often only the lawyers profited.

Cases turned on many technicalities of tithe law, but two issues stand out in the disputes of the late eighteenth century. First, moduses came under renewed attack and, second, tithe owners attempted to establish their rights to 'new' crops such as potatoes and turnips. Both issues arose from the quickening pace of agricultural change at the end of the eighteenth century. More farmers and landowners were claiming that either their lands, or particular animals or crops, were protected by customary payments, but few found it easy to satisfy the precise requirements of the law.[11] As agricultural prosperity grew, tithe owners made something of a concerted attempt to destroy such customs and substitute more realistic equivalents. An apologist for the Church of England noted in 1782 that during the previous thirty years the clergy 'have been more attentive and better informed and have therefore made a considerable progress in augmenting their composition for tithes'.[12] A 'Member of the Church of England' complained to the Bishop of Lincoln in 1792 that the Church had been 'suffered to stir dormant claims so antiquated, that all memory and evidence of the original transaction are gone'.[13] The introduction of new crops – sainfoins, turnips and potatoes – also excited the interest of the tithe owners. They could hardly ignore developments which would deprive them of income if the farmers successfully established the point that by custom new crops were not tithable. There were many legal disputes, including a bitter and protracted one in Hornchurch (Essex),[14] which arose from the development of the potato market to supply growing urban centres.

Most tithe cases were heard either in the diocesan church courts or in the equity courts of Chancery and Exchequer. Church courts provided the speedier jurisdiction, but were naturally pre-disposed towards the rights of the Church. They were widely condemned as anachronistic, but they preserved a more or less effective jurisdiction over tithe, matrimonial and morality causes well into the second half of the eighteenth century. Equity courts were very expensive and dilatory. The Kendal tithe dispute, for example, lasted from 1817 to 1834, and even then was determined not by an equity court but by private Act of Parliament. It cost the protagonists over £20,000.[15] Admittedly this was exceptional, but costs which ran into thousands rather than hundreds frightened would-be litigants into disadvantageous out-of-court settlements. The power of the purse was a vital factor in the outcome of the contests[16] and, in the words of one frustrated Staffordshire rector beaten by superior forces, *Might* frequently overcame *Right*.[17]

Although tithe disputes are as old as the tithe system itself, the question of Commutation was not seriously discussed until the beginning of the nineteenth century. Five reasons seem to account for this. First, British agriculture became much more efficient in the eighteenth and early nineteenth centuries. 'Improvement' was the dominant theme, reiterated remorselessly in the newly-founded agricultural magazines such as *Annals of Agriculture, Farmers Magazine*, and the *Bath and West of England Agricultural Society Journal*, and intoned fervently by the arch-priests Arthur Young, William Marshall and Sir James Sinclair. To a man, the agricultural improvers condemned the tithe system as an obstacle to improvement. Second, the enclosure movement of *c*.1760 to *c*.1820, an integral part of this improvement campaign, offered three realistic solutions to the tithe problem – land in lieu of tithe, straight cash payments, or payments varying with prevailing corn prices.[18] Third, the Church of England was coming under increasing pressure to reform itself. Alongside nepotism, pluralities and non-residence, tithes figured prominently in the reformers' campaign. By the 1830s, many leading churchmen and politicians, such as Sir Robert Peel, saw reform or disestablishment as incontrovertible choices. In such a climate, graceful concessions on tithe, however strenuously resisted earlier, were a small price to pay for preserving the specially privileged status of the Church of England.

Fourth, there was in the 1830s a more generalized impetus for reform in many spheres. The ice had been broken in 1828-9 with Catholic Emancipation and the repeal of the Test and Corporations Acts. The 1832 Reform Act set the scene for a 'decade of reform'. The Commutation Act flanks and complements two major administration reforms – the establishment of the Poor Law Commission in 1834 and Civil Registration from 1837 – and all three were integral parts of the process whereby government responsibilities were extended and a centralized bureaucracy created. Nor was the Tithe Commutation Act an isolated example of ecclesiastical reform. A Royal Commission, which Peel's short minority government of 1834-5 had established to consider Church reform, bore substantial fruit under Lord Melbourne's Whig administration. Acts of 1836, 1838 and 1840[19] rationalized both episcopal geography and incomes, attacked the menace of pluralism, and made a substantial contribution towards redistributing the income of the Church in favour of its poorly beneficed ministers.[20] As with tithe, such reforms were much overdue, and though they revealed in a rather brutal way the powers that Parliament held over the Established Church, they paradoxically served to strengthen rather than weaken the bonds between them. A decade which had begun with real likelihood of disestablishment ended quietly for the Church with its critics appeased or frustrated and its status secured. Rarely has a policy of tactical retreat reaped such strategic rewards. Considered in this context, therefore, even such a far-reaching measure as the Tithe Commutation Act fits naturally into a climate of change. It would not have been possible before 1830.

The fifth factor is a short-term one: tithe commutation was enacted during a period of agricultural depression. There were no fewer than five parliamentary select committees enquiring into agricultural distress between 1820 and 1836. The last two, in 1833 and 1836, heard much evidence from an over-taxed farming community oppressed in particular by poor-rate assessments and tithes. The extent of the depression may have been exaggerated, as modern agricultural historians have suggested, but a Parliament still composed very largely of landowners even after 1832 was not deaf to the cry that food producers were discriminated against in comparison with industrialists and manufacturers.

Of the five reasons listed above, the first – agricultural improvement – was undoubtedly the most important in generating the necessary momentum for change. Agricultural improvement was essential to meet the demands of a population growing at an unprecedented rate, especially as, from the 1780s if not earlier, a significantly smaller proportion of the workforce was engaged in farming. This was not the main argument which swayed contemporaries, however. Their great imperative was profit. After a mid-century period in the doldrums, especially for arable farmers, prices and profits picked up from the 1760s. The period of the French wars (1793-1815) was one of unprecedented boom for British farmers, and the proliferating magazines and journals were full of helpful hints on how to increase profitability by investment in improvements. All hindrances, from lazy overpaid labourers to open-field farms, were castigated remorselessly. Tithe, listed by Adam Smith as one of the 'effectual bars' to efficient husbandry,[21] received its full share of obloquy. Smith pointed out that it operated as a differential tax. As tithe represented a tenth of the gross rather than the net produce, it operated the more severely on those poorer quality lands where improvement was most necessary. 'Upon the rent of rich lands, the tythe may sometimes be a tax of no more than one-fifth part, or four shillings in the pound; whereas on that of poorer lands it may sometimes be a tax of one half, or ten shillings in the pound.'[22] Sir James Sinclair made similar calculations in 1803,[23] and the pages of agricultural and other magazines frequently carried stories of improvement frustrated by the exorbitant demands of the tithe owner. William Cobbett, for example, was told how a farmer, after making valiant and initially successful efforts to improve soils in the Mendip Hills, was deterred from further operations by a tithe demand of 10s. per acre in the first year of cultivation.[24] If tithes were taken in kind, or by realistic compositions during a period of improvement, it followed also that increases in tithe revenue outstripped rent rises. Expressed another way, tithe represented an ever greater proportion of the rental value. An agriculturalist calculated that in a district of his acquaintance rents had risen by 40 per cent in the forty years after 1792 while tithes had risen by 140 per cent. The Rev. Richard Jones, soon to be one of the three tithe commissioners, suggested in 1836 that evidence such as this had concentrated men's minds on the need for commutation: 'It is natural ... that this different rate of progress in the clergyman's income and in his own should be distasteful to the landowner; that he should see with aversion the proprietor of what he considers a subordinate interest in the soil, acquiring from it revenues approaching by successive steps nearer and nearer to his own.'[25]

There is no doubt that the improvers overstated their case against tithes. As the Rev. Morgan Cove sourly observed: 'Every shaft which ingenuity, wit or malice could devise hath been levelled against them insomuch as there is hardly an imaginary or real grievance with which this country is so pathetically said to be oppressed which hath not been attributed to the payment of tithes.'[26] The extent to which tithes operated as a deterrent, however, does not affect this argument.[27] Most contemporaries were persuaded to believe that they deterred massively and that the deterrence was particularly serious when the country was fighting for its existence against a French nation which was trying to starve it into submission and when a rapidly growing – and increasingly urbanised – population needed to be fed. Here, as in so many other spheres of political life, the French wars initially dampened prospects for reform while making radical change the more likely when the immediate danger had passed.

The necessity for commutation had become accepted by the 1830s. As *The Times* observed in 1834, 'All men of all parties express the most anxious desire to see the tithe question set at rest.'[28] The banner of tithe reform in the colder climate of the 1810s had been carried by the wealthy Cumbrian mine-owner and practical farmer, John Christian Curwen, Whig M.P. for Carlisle. Coming from the extreme north-west, he had practical experience of the disincentive effects of tithing in kind and his opposition took the practical path of an attack on obstacles to agricultural improvement.[29] In 1816, Curwen persuaded the Commons to appoint a Select Committee 'to report to the House if it be expedient to enable the Owners of Tithes and Occupiers of Tithable Lands and others to substitute pecuniary payments for Tithes in kind during certain specified periods.'[30] In 1817 Curwen's attempts to help farmers prove fixed modus payments against attacks on them by tithe-owners were defeated by a Tory majority which paid heed to the arguments of the tithe-owning University of Cambridge: 'The law of tithes is interwoven with the Constitution, no less of the State than of the Church and has been guaranteed by every Charter of our Civil Liberties.'[31]

The first Bill to commute tithes on a national basis was introduced by another M.P. from the north-west, Thomas Greene of Lancaster, in 1828. Commutation was to be permissive only, on the assent of landowners, tithe owners and the relevant diocesan bishop. It was based on Greene's experience in seeing contentious tithe disputes at Lancaster and nearby Cockerham settled by private Acts of Parliament in 1824 and 1825;[32] but in proposing fluctuating corn rents it also echoed a scheme favoured by Pitt the Younger when he toyed with tithe reform in 1791-2.

In the debate on Greene's Bill, Sir Robert Peel defended the interests of his Oxford University constituents and insisted that commutation arrangements should last no longer than twenty-one years.[33] It was noticeable, however, that outright opposition to interference with tithe property was much more muted than previously. Though Greene's Bill was lost, the climate of opinion had shifted and the tithe question was regularly debated in Parliament between 1828 and 1836.

The case for tithe reform was strengthened by the agricultural disturbances in the south of England in 1830-31. Agricultural labourers' protests for higher wages were often deflected by landowners and farmers who argued that they could not afford to pay more in view of the heavy demands of the titheman. Between sixty and seventy 'Swing' disturbances seem to have centred around the tithe payments.[34] Parliament received numerous petitions between 1829 and 1831 calling for tithe reform.[35] These were carefully orchestrated in the Commons by the radical M.P. for Aberdeen, Joseph Hume, and in the Upper House by Lord King. Hume argued that compulsory provision for clerics was counter-productive.[36] Very few Members would follow him down an avenue which led to abolition rather than commutation. The Church itself, however, realized that movement on the tithe issue was essential. In 1830, Archbishop Howley introduced a permissive Bill to reform the tithe system by encouraging long leases, and by 1832 Henry Ryder, Bishop of Lichfield and Coventry, stated in his charge to the clergy of his diocese that he was prepared to consider permanent commutation in order to 'relieve the intercourse between the Minister and the bulk of his people from occasions of collision' and to restore 'a right pastoral and spiritual feeling between the shepherd and his flock'.[37] If the dignitaries of the Church had any will to resist proposals for commutation, it was sapped by the extraordinarily violent reaction to the Lords' rejection of the second parliamentary reform Bill in 1831. All but five of the 26 bishops voted against reform, and the riots and demonstrations which followed in Derby, Bristol, Nottingham and elsewhere were vituperatively anticlerical in tone.[38]

The road to tithe commutation was prepared by important concessions to farmers and landowners brought before the Courts for non-payment of tithe dues. Lord Tenterden's Act of 1832 decreed that defenders of moduses need only prove continuous payment for thirty years to have them established by law. This cut through the enormously complicated rules for the establishment of a modus which, in general, worked to the advantage of tithe owners.[39] An Act of 1834 prevented tithe owners from making claims for tithes which had not been collected at any time in the previous sixty years;[40] and in 1835 small claims of £10 or less were made recoverable only in magistrates' courts, thus closing the door to punitive and expensive claims in the equity courts.[41] Ironically, Tenterden's Act inflamed the very passions it was designed to cool. It gave plaintiffs a year in which to pursue claims without hindrance. The result was a flood of litigation, which did much to revive radical appetite for the fight against the Church.

Three unsuccessful commutation Bills, in 1833, 1834 and 1835, preceded the Act of 1836. The 1833 Bill was introduced by Lord Althorp, Chancellor of the Exchequer. It allowed for compulsory commutation unless the parties could agree voluntarily within a year. The basis of commutation was to be a corn rent determined by the value of tithe receipts during the seven years immediately preceding commutation. The Conservative opposition, led by Sir Robert Peel, opposed the compulsory clauses. There were also many objections on points of detail from the Whig side, and Althorp eventually decided that such a complex measure should await maturer reflection in the next session.

The Chancellor's second tithe commutation Bill followed a Commons Committee report in April 1834 'that it is expedient to effect a Commutation of Tithes and to abolish the collection and payment of Tithes in kind throughout England and Wales and in lieu thereof to substitute an annual payment to the Parties entitled to Tithes.'[42] The Bill paid much greater attention to local problems than its predecessor had done. A separate valuation of land in each county was proposed, and tithe was to be expressed as apermanently fixed proportion of the rent of the land from which the tithe fell due. This proportion was to be determined at Quarter Sessions, after detailed consideration of soil quality and land use. There was also provision, in certain circumstances, for redemption of tithes at twenty-five years' purchase. Tithe had been calculated in some parishes as a fixed proportion of rent, but the practice was not a common one and there was some resistance to such a formulation, despite the advantages of local experience which the Bill would bring into play. The Bill was eventually withdrawn to permit more Parliamentary time to be made available for discussion of the yet more vexatious issue of Irish tithes.[43] The Established Church remained implacably opposed to compulsory commutation, the otherwise tractable Archbishop Howley indicating to Lord John Russell that he would oppose any tithe bill which coerced the clergy.[44]

The Church hoped for more compassionate treatment from Sir Robert Peel's minority Conservative Government. Peel's Tamworth Manifesto of December 1834 had unequivocally indicated his desire to achieve tithe commutation 'founded upon just principles and proposed after mature deliberation'.[45] His Bill, introduced in March 1835, showed evidence enough of 'mature deliberation' and also of profit from the experience of Althorp's efforts. The Conservatives could not countenance compulsion, but in the clauses of this voluntary Bill are to be found the genesis of Russell's successful measure of 1836. Peel reverted to the 1833 scheme of a corn rent, varying with the price of wheat, barley and oats. The corn rent could be revised, if changed agricultural circumstances warranted it, after seven years. Agreement to effect commutation was to be signified by not less than two-thirds of the tithe owners and tithe payers by value. The agreement itself had to be scrutinized by tithe commissioners to ensure that there was no collusion between the parties and that the general principles of the Bill had not been flouted.

The Irish situation drove Peel from office less than a month after the Bill was introduced, so that it was impossible to test the arguments voiced in debate that a voluntary Bill would attract few takers among tithe owners.[46]

Chapter II

THE ACT OF 1836

The Whigs, of course, were committed to introducing compulsory commutation. Lord John Russell, as Home Secretary, was given the unenviable task of attempting to pilot yet another tithe Bill through Parliament. He acknowledged to the House that no Bill could deal with all the complexities of the issue, and he expressed himself willing to consider constructive amendments. His objective was to produce 'as little disturbance as possible to existing interests',[47] but he insisted that although commutation was ideally to be achieved by agreement, if that failed compulsion was required.

The passage of the Bill through Parliament shows clearly enough that the Whigs were open to persuasion on all points of detail. The original Bill was greatly extended.[48] In particular, the clauses dealing with expenses attendant on the collection of tithes were extensively amended. Russell originally proposed (Bill, cl. 29) that collection expenses should always fall between 25 per cent and 40 per cent of the gross value of the tithe. *The Times* saw the clause as an act of spoilation, the proceeds of which would go directly into the pockets of the landlords.[49] Russell, after a considerable fight, gave way: the amended clause allowed assistant commissioners discretion to fix whatever deduction for collection expenses seemed appropriate in the circumstances. Russell's attempt to fix an additional rent charge of 15s. 0d. an acre when land was newly cultivated with hops was also defeated in committee. A new clause was substituted, which introduced the concept of 'ordinary' and 'extraordinary' rent charge on hop grounds and market gardens, the precise rate of extraordinary rent charge per acre being left to the discretion of the assistant commissioners. The general tendency of the amendments, indeed, was to shy away from precise statements about tithe value, and to enable assistant commissioners to exercise flexibility in harmony with varying local conditions. Because the Whigs wanted as much support for the measure as possible, they had to compromise and conciliate. Thomas Pemberton, M.P. for Ripon, remarked that the amended Bill 'was so little the same that the supporters of the Government were now called upon to vote for the very measure which the former night they had repudiated'.[50] This was pardonable exaggeration, but it did indicate that the Government's main concern was to get tithe commutation onto the Statute Book. Precise details could be amended, or left to be decided on the ground by local representatives of the tithe commission. Lord John Russell was content that many of the criticisms cancelled each other out. As the Bill had been called both 'a clergyman's Bill' and 'a landlord's Bill', it seemed to him reasonable to assume that the Government had steered the appropriate middle course.[51]

The House of Lords offered little opposition to the Bill. The bishops, however, insisted that they should see each agreement relating to clerical tithes before the tithe commissioners confirmed it. The Bill, much amended in the Commons, went quietly through the Lords, the bishops being by now sure that peaceable commutation offered them their best chance of seeing tithes converted into more desirable and secure property without significant loss. The Bill received the Royal Assent as the Tithe Commutation Act[52] on 13 August 1836.

The bureaucratic structure created to solve the tithe problem was closely modelled on Peel's abortive 1835 scheme and also on the Poor Law Commission established in 1834. At the apex of the structure were the three tithe commissioners, working from London. Two were appointed by the Crown – in practice the Home Secretary – and one by the Archbishop of Canterbury (cl.1). The commissioners appointed the secretariat as well as the assistant commissioners who were to be the commissioners' representatives in the field (cl.4). The salaries of the tithe commissioners, their assistants and other officers were paid from the public purse and not by the parties to tithe commutation (cl.7). The first tithe commissioners were William Blamire, a nephew of John Christian Curwen and, like him, Whig M.P. for a Cumberland seat; Captain T. Wentworth Buller; and, appointed by the Archbishop of Canterbury, the Rev. Richard Jones. Blamire was the dominant commissioner. He had considerable experience of tithe matters in Cumberland and Westmorland and Peel acknowledged in March 1836 that he had made the ablest contribution to the debate on Russell's Bill.[53] On taking office Blamire had to resign his seat in Parliament, since no commissioner or assistant commissioner could serve as an M.P. (cl.5). Wentworth Buller, a keen agriculturalist with interests in Devon and Northampton, owed his appointment to the patronage of Russell. He was an active Whig supporter in the south-west. The Rev. Richard Jones had published two pamphlets on the tithe question in 1833 and 1836, and had held the Chair of Political Economy at King's College, London.[54]

The Act gave the commissioners the power to confirm voluntary agreements on tithes and to frame compulsory agreements; but it allowed (cl.11) such powers to be delegated to assistant commissioners. In practice, of course, they usually were. Assistant commissioners became the 'restless shuttles' of the commutation machinery, as they scurried from one parish to another, offering advice, settling disputes, confirming agreements and effecting compulsory commutation. The main burden in over 12,000 tithe districts was carried by men such as John Job Rawlinson, Thomas S. Woolley, Charles Pym, Horace W. Meteyard, Charles Howard, George Cooke and Joseph Townsend. Each supervised well over a hundred commutations and, in doing so, demonstrated a high degree of resourcefulness, initiative and skill. Most assistants had been land agents or valuers, so that their professional skills were relevant to their work for the Commission. Some, in fact, spent most of their working lives first as enclosure commissioners and then with the Tithe Commission. The commissioners preferred their assistants to be full-time appointments. For example, in 1837 Joseph Townsend of Wood End near Marlow (Bucks) gave up employment as a land agent and enclosure commissioner, worth over £500 a year, to become an assistant tithe commisioner. He worked on several hundred commutations between 1837 and 1851. Before he was appointed, Richard Jones asked pertinent questions about Townsend's availability: 'I have some reason for wishing to know if in the event of your being appointed an assistant commissioner you could give up all your time to the service of the commissioners and whether you could conveniently reside near London.'[55]

One of the most onerous jobs which the Act gave assistant commissioners was the resolution of disputes over moduses or other liability to payment of tithe (cl.45). These were the very issues which had plunged parishes into acrimony for years, and the Commutation Act empowered commissioners 'to appoint a Time and Place in or near the parish for hearing and determining the same.' Assistant commissioners' decisions were subject to the usual appeals at law (cl.46), but these were rarely invoked. Usually the assistant commissioner heard the evidence on both sides, reached his decision and, if a modus were established, incorporated its details in the tithe apportionment so that there could be no further occasion for dispute. One assistant commissioner, John Herbert, told the Select Committee on the Enclosure and Improvement of Commons in 1844 that he had been called upon to make 148 decisions concerning doubtful tithe rights and only 10 of these had been subject to appeal.[56] Richard Jones approved the fact that the assistant commissioners were able to bring 'justice to the door'. In view of the fact that tithe disputes had been so common and so contentious before 1836, their happy resolution by assistant commissioners may be seen as one of the most important successes of the Act.

The Act made provision for both voluntary and compulsory tithe commutation. Voluntary agreements followed fairly closely the procedure for enclosures. Owners of not less than one-quarter of either the lands or tithes of a parish could call a parochial meeting to discuss commutation (cl.17). At that meeting, any sum in lieu of tithes agreed by two-thirds of the landowners by value and by two-thirds of both great and small tithe owners was binding on the remainder of the parish. Thus, as for enclosures, one large landowner could override the wishes of the parish. Every voluntary agreement had to be approved by the bishop of the diocese (cl.28) and the patron of the living (cl.26) before the assistant commissioner, having ensured it had been made 'without Fraud or Collusion' (cl.27), recommended it for the commissioners' approval.

Once a voluntary agreement had been confirmed, a meeting of landowners was necessary to appoint a valuer to apportion the agreed rent-charge on each plot of land (cl.32-33). This involved the compilation of maps and plans, though old maps could be used if the valuer thought it proper and three-quarters of the landowners by value agreed (cl.35). The cost of all apportionments, both of voluntary and compulsory commutations, was to be met by landowners alone, in proportion to the rateable value of their land (cl.75). Other expenses of land surveyors and tithe valuers 'necessary for making any Award' were to be borne by land and tithe owners 'in such Proportion Time and Manner as the Commissioner shall direct' (cl.74).

Compulsory commutations were to begin after 1 October 1838, thus giving parties two years in which to reach voluntary agreement (cl.36). Assistant commissioners were to ascertain the value of tithes each year between 1829 and 1835, with no deductions for payment of parochial and county rates (cl.37). Commissioners were, however, to estimate the value of these taxes in making their Award for, whatever the practice before commutation, tithe owners were henceforward to be responsible for paying taxes on their rent charge. If one half of the landowners or tithe owners by value made representation that the average payments from 1829 to 1835 did not 'fairly represent the Sum which ought to be taken for calculating a permanent commutation of the Great or Small Tithes ... the Commissioner shall have power to diminish the sum to be so taken by a sum amounting to not more than one-fifth part of the average value ascertained as aforesaid' (cl.38). Commissioners thus had a 20 per cent leeway which was widely used to adjust tithe values, usually upwards. There was also provision (cl.39) for special adjudication of the value of tithes in exceptional cases – for example, where a tithe owner had been defrauded of his proper dues. In such cases, the commissioners were to calculate tithe values 'having regard to the average rate which shall be awarded in respect of lands of the like Description and similarly situated in the neighbouring Parishes'.

These tithe values were converted into rent charge payments by assuming that each sum had been used to purchase equal quantities of wheat, barley and oats at prices published annually in the *London Gazette* (cl.56-57). The scale was first fixed in December 1836 when £100 of tithe would purchase 94.95 bushels of wheat, 168.42 of barley and 242.42 of oats. These calculations were used by valuers throughout the country to obtain the initial rent charge, and the figures appear at the end of the preamble to each tithe apportionment.

Procedure for recovering rent charge was also stated clearly in the Act. If payment had not been made within 21 days of falling due, the tithe owner could enter the defaulter's lands and distrain for the amount outstanding (cl.81). If this proved impossible, the sheriff would issue a writ taking possession of the defaulter's property until the debt was discharged (cl.82). Prior to 1836, one of the main problems in recovering tithe debts had been doubt over the amount due. Tithe rent-charge liability was precisely calculated and thus more easily recovered.

There was provision in the Act for certain tithe produce which could not be commuted according to a national average. Hops, fruit and garden produce were to be separately valued (cl.40), as was coppice wood (cl.41). Hops and market-garden tithes posed a specific problem since they tended to be particularly valuable and would distort the rent charge if lands were converted, for example, to hop grounds or if they ceased to be cultivated as such. The Tithe Act (cl.42) distinguished between ordinary and extra-ordinary rent charge. The extraordinary rent charge was to be a rate per acre, settled by the commissioners on hops and market gardens which could be removed from the total rent charge if less profitable crops were subsequently to be sown.

Two further points are worthy of note. A few tithes, not usually payable in most parts of the country, remained uncommuted. Personal tithes and tithe of fish were excluded (cl.90), as were Easter offerings, mortuaries and surplice fees. These latter categories were not strictly tithes at all but had been computed as such in many parishes. Secondly, rent-charge payments were declared to be the responsibility of landowners rather than tenants (cl.80). The common practice of asking the tenant to make rent-charge payments with an appropriate rental adjustment continued, but tenants could no longer be prosecuted for non-payment.

The 1836 Tithe Commutation Act remained the essential statement on rent-charge conversion until 1936. It did, however, require amendment on points of detail in the few years after its passage. Three Acts, passed in 1838, 1839 and 1846, deserve special notice. In 1838 an Act was passed to facilitate merger of tithes in land:[57] those who owned the tithes of their own land were enabled to merge two properties and thus extinguish rent charge altogether. A 'merger' was a legally binding declaration that the value of tithe had been subsumed in that of the land from which it fell due. Thus those who were fortunate enough to own the tithes of their own land could merge the one property with the other and thus extinguish tithe and rent charge altogether. Mergers proved popular, since they avoided the trouble and expense of valuations, maps and apportionments. Certain tithe districts were exonerated from tithe entirely by mergers. By 1851, 13,160 mergers had been enrolled by the tithe commissioners. An Act 'to explain and amend the Acts for the Commutation of Tithes' was passed in 1839.[58] This enabled mergers of tithe with glebe land to be effected, and agreements could also be made to commute Easter offerings and other charges not within the scope of the 1836 Act. The 1846 Tithe Amendment Act[59] was passed on the initiative of the tithe commissioners who anticipated difficulties which would arise when nearly all tithes had been extinguished, but the few remaining charges necessitated full commutation at disproportionate expense. The Act, therefore, permitted landowners to redeem rent values of £15 or less at 24 years' purchase.

Chapter III

THE ACT IN PRACTICE

By any standards, the work of the Tithe Commission was discharged with commendable efficiency. In the space of sixteen years, from 1836 to 1852, it effected one of the major redistributions of English property. Given the rancour which tithe had traditionally generated, the speed and success of commutations were little short of remarkable. Yet the Commission's very efficiency has invited neglect. Unlike its better-known counterpart, the Poor Law Commission, the Tithe Commission did not stir up controversy wherever it went. Nor did it have a didactic and overweening publicist like Edwin Chadwick at its head. As a result, while the Poor Law Commission excited fevered comment in all the newspapers and wreaked havoc in much of the north of England, the Tithe Commission went quietly and industriously about its work, generating in the process little of the juicy raw material good for publicity. It may be objected that the Poor Law was an inherently more important and contentious subject affecting rural and urban areas alike, and a life-and-death issue to boot. There is obviously some truth in this, and one can understand why social historians have concentrated on the Poor Law and neglected Tithe. Yet no one who has studied the tithe system would be prepared to write it off as at most a minor local irritant. Improperly handled, in the way that the Poor Law Commission assuredly was, commutation would have unleashed a fury of resentment and recrimination, filling the pages of newspapers read by the propertied classes. The work of the tithe commissioners deserves to be considered an integral part of the 'growth of government' which characterised the middle years of the nineteenth century. Administrative and social historians alike have unjustly neglected it.[60]

The tithe commissioners divided the country into 12,275 districts. In many cases, especially for voluntary agreements, the parish was the tithe district. Sometimes, however, it was necessary to divide large parishes, with varied land-use or difficult tithe problems, into as many as twenty districts for the purposes of compulsory commutation. In several northern counties, such as Lancashire, the township was the usual unit for tithe administration. By 1852 the commissioners had confirmed tithe apportionments, which parcelled out the rent charge on individual plots of land, in 11,395 districts (92.83 per cent).[61] The remaining cases, some of which dragged on into the 1880s, were mostly those in which most tithes had already been exonerated, for example at enclosure, and proprietors were unwilling to bear the expense of surveying and mapping an entire district for the sake of rent charge of a few pounds. In some cases, the tithe commissioners were trying to engineer merger declarations from landowners who also owned the tithes of their estates. At Great Claybrook (Leics.), for example, the commissioners noted in their 1851 Report to Parliament that all tithes except those of pigs (worth £1) and from a Mill (5s.) had been long since exonerated. 'To establish rent charges of 25/- and to proceed by map and apportionment to finish the commutation would be a harsh and burdensome proceeding.'[62] In the huge parish of Leek (Staffordshire) which spread over 25,000 acres, most landowners owned their own tithes. The commissioners naturally wished to postpone commutation in the various districts until declarations of merger under the 1838 Act had been signed by as many proprietors as possible. Eventually only £5 2s. 6d. was apportioned as rent charge throughout the parish, though commutation was delayed in six of the twelve districts until 1851-3. In Leek and Lowe district, for example, assistant commissioner Charles Pym waited from 1845, when he began proceedings for compulsory commutation, until 1851 for merger declarations from all 53

LANDOWNERS.	OCCUPIERS.	TOTAL QUANTITIES.	RENT-CHARGE PAYABLE TO *Vicar of Hutton*			RENT-CHARGE PAYABLE TO *Impropriators in equal Moieties*		
		A. R. P.	£.	s.	d.	£.	s.	d.

(i) Extract from the summary of the Marton Tithe Apportionment

proprietors to be signed.[63] Commutation at Huncoat, a township of some 600 acres in the parish of Whalley (Lancs.), could not be confirmed until the commissioners had persuaded the curate and landowners to take advantage of the 1846 Tithe Amendment Act. Eventually, in May 1853, the parties agreed to redeem the outstanding tithe payment of £1 for £29 9s. 0d.[64]

Of the 11,395 apportionments confirmed by 1852, 7,147 (62.72 per cent) were of voluntary agreements. This was a considerably higher proportion than most of the Whig M.P.s had believed possible in 1836. The tithe commissioners naturally favoured voluntary agreements, since they were quicker, cheaper, and easier to arrange. Voluntary commutation was mostly effected in the late 1830s and early 1840s. The original intention had been to close the door to voluntary agreements two years after the Act came into operation, but this was recognised as impracticable. Only 77 per cent of voluntary agreements had been confirmed by 1840. The voluntary process had been virtually completed by 1844 with 98 per cent of agreements confirmed. The majority of compulsory commutations (82.14 per cent) were arranged between 1839 and 1847, with peak years in 1842-6.

Parties were left considerable latitude in coming to a voluntary agreement. They were not to be hampered by precise calculations of averages, though they had to satisfy an assistant commissioner that their agreement was fair and unforced. Assistant commissioners were asked to make their own valuations of the tithes. Only very rarely did they fail to recommend the commissioners to accept the agreement, even if there was a significant disparity between the parties. It was one of the great strengths of the Commission – and one conspicuously not shared by the Poor Law Commissioners – that it was prepared to be flexible in order to achieve harmony. On voluntary agreements, it almost invariably took the view that the interested parties knew their own business better than an assistant commissioner, coming as a stranger to a parish, could ever know it. An agreement voluntarily achieved it took as *prima facie* evidence of reasonableness. The commissioners reported in 1837 that they had rejected only 16 of the first 374 agreements submitted to them.[65] In eight cases they accepted their assistants' view that the rent charge was grossly inadequate, considering the levels of neighbouring parishes; in seven the parties had not computed the level of rates that the tithe owner would have to pay after commutation; and the final case turned on a technical dispute about the alteration of a rent charge after agreement. It will be noted that on no occasion did the commissioners consider reducing the level of an agreement.

The commissioners confirmed several agreements even when their assistants had considerable reservations. J. J. Rawlinson, commenting on an agreement to commute the tithes of Netherwasdale, Eskdale and Wasdale (Cumberland), said that, although his valuation had been £165, and an agreement had been reached at £134, he would recommend acceptance. 'The bargain has been made by parties who were fully aware what they were about.'[66] T. S. Wooley also recommended the commissioners to accept a voluntary agreement at Chatham (Kent) to give the rector £808, although a valuation had suggested the tithes to be worth £987, after deducting all collection expenses.[67] Assistant Commissioner A. O. Baker noted that the agreement at Longstock (Hants.) had been 'arrived at in a very unusual manner'. However, as all parties had 'agreed to its adoption, I am not prepared to say that its fairness can be questioned'.[68]

There is some evidence, however, that assistant commissioners took special care that the interests of the Church were not harmed. Agreements made by lay impropriators were assumed to emanate from men of business; clerics might not have the acumen to stand up to determined proprietors. Thomas Sudworth, in accepting the agreement at Whittington (Staffs.), noted that 'The great tithes of Whittington being now under Lease ... I presume that they (not having much land in the parish) will have made the best bargain they could with the landowners'.[69] George Ashdown recommended acceptance of the Bilbrooke (Staffs.), agreement although his valuation of the tithe was higher than the sum agreed. He reported: 'If these tithes were Ecclesiastical rather than lay I should not recommend this agreement to be confirmed until there is a further enquiry'.[70] The commissioners did insist that an agreement for rent charge of £13 12s. 10d. at Elford (Staffs.), where most tithes had been commuted for land at enclosure in 1766, should be increased to £30 1s. 10d. R. B. Phillipson reported that the agreement seemed unfair to the rector: 'The late Rector was an elderly man, and was content to take the old composition, and the present Rector told me he was quite ignorant of the value of the tithes'.[71]

Most of the assistant commissioners' time was taken up in arranging compulsory commutations when the parties concerned could not agree on an appropriate sum. In this task, they followed fairly precise instructions issued by the commissioners in a circular entitled *Course of Proceeding in Making Awards*.[72] It was crucial to discover the tithe receipts for the years of average (1829-35), and also to enquire whether there were any grounds for varying the sum thus obtained. It was necessary also to discover what rates and taxes were due, since after commutation the tithe owner was formally charged with their payment. Before 1836 arrangements for payment of rates on tithes had been haphazard and various.

The success of the assistant commissioners in arranging compulsory commutations may be gauged by the fact that there was little opposition to their decisions. Appeals against tithe awards were rare and, perhaps more surprisingly, their decisions on modus disputes were also regularly accepted. Assistant commissioners did have to advise some meetings which turned into unseemly wrangles, but an accommodation was usually

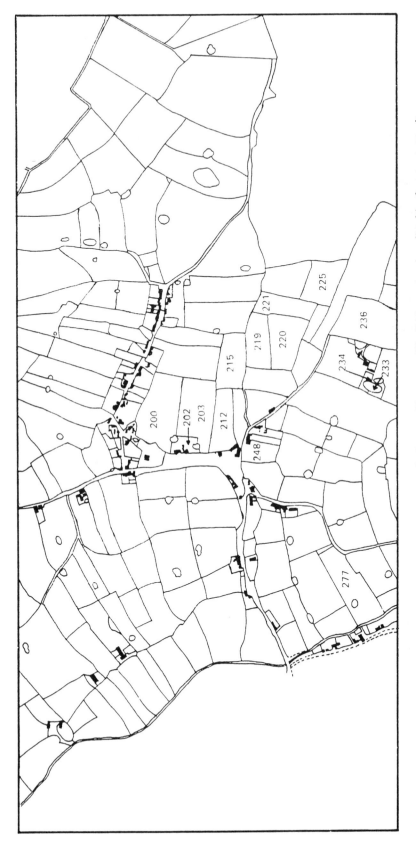

(ii) Section drawn from Tithe Award Map for Marton in the County of Lancaster. The fields numbered are listed in the extract opposite. All fields in the original map are numbered.

LANDOWNERS	OCCUPIERS	Number referring to the Plan	NAME AND DESCRIPTION of LANDS AND PREMISES	STATE of CULTIVATION	QUANTITIES in STATUTE MEASURE			Amount of Rent Charge apportioned upon the several lands, and to whom payable. PAYABLE TO VICAR			PAYABLE TO [co-proprietors]		
					a.	r.	p.	£	s.	d.	£	s.	d.
Hall Margaret	William Andrews	202	House, garden &c	Pasture	"	2	29	"	1	4	"	"	10
		200	do		5	1	15	"	2	1	"	"	1
		203	do	Arable	4	2	29	"	2	1	"	12	1
		212	Maids acre		2	"	34	"	1	1	"	5	9
		215	Mercer Meadow	Meadow	8	"	"	"	1	14	"	7	10
		219	Haddon Meadow		2	1	34	"	1	6	"	6	6
		240	East Croft	Arable	1	"	3	"	"	5	"	2	6
		655	Marsh Field		3	1	12	"	1	3	"	6	4
		656			1	2	34	"	1	4	"	3	2
		241	Great Slate field	Pasture	4	1	10	"	1	4	"	10	10
					20	3	12	13			3	0	10
Ashton Thomas Boddon	Thomas Jolly	236	House &c	Meadow	1	"	16	1	"	0	"	"	10
		233	Stack Yard		1	1	24	1	"	2	"	1	9
		234	do		1	"	13	1	"	2	"	8	9
		220	Great Haddon Meadow	Meadow	3	1	7	1	"	5	"	5	10
		221	Connot field	Arable	2	"	30	1	"	11	"	3	10
		223	Flurtly &c	Meadow	1	1	33	1	"	0	"	10	5
		227	Broom &c	Arable	4	"	15	2	2	9	"	13	5
		280	Laws	"	5	1	4	2	"	2	"	6	10
		229	Haddon	Pasture	2	2	20	2	1	5	"	0	9
		230	Haddon Tops		3	1	25	3	1	5	"	12	11
		231	East Haddon	"	6	"	17	2	2	7½	"	9	2
		232	South Haddon	"	3	2	33	1	2	6	"	7	10
		235	West Haddon	"	3	"	13	1	1	4	"	0	0
		237	Long Haddon &c	Arable	0	1	19	2	2	10	"	19	0
		297	Summers fields	Pasture	4	3	19	1	1	0	"	12	0
		298	Meadow field	Meadow	2	3	24	1	1	6	"	2	3
		300	Set field	"	3	2	"	1	1	5	"	1	1
					50	2	34	1	5	1	4	4	"

(iii) *Extract from the Marton Tithe Apportionment showing rent charge to be apportioned field by field for each proprietor.*

reached. A note of weariness often crept into the assistant commissioners' reports to Whitehall, however, as they recount the story of disputes thrashed out at commutation meetings. John Johnes, for example, had to arbitrate between landowners, impropriator and vicar at Ambleton (Pembroke). The landowner objected to the impropriator's averages, and succeeded in having them reduced from £151 10s. 5d. to £147 15s. 9d. The impropriator claimed the full 20 per cent increase on the averages; the landowners offered 10 per cent. Eventually, Johnes, after taking advice from his superiors, settled the rent charge to the impropriator at £170, an increase of 15.03 per cent on his receipts during the years of average. After much haggling, the rent charge due to the vicar was settled at £141 12s. 9d., a full 20 per cent higher than the average sum received by him between 1829 and 1835.[73] At Begelly, Johnes was met with a claim from the rector to set aside the average receipt of £204 8s. ¾d. altogether, and to institute a separate adjudication, 'but the only evidence he adduced to support his argument was that the Rector was one of those clergymen who wished to live on terms with his parishioners, and was a good man, that he raised the tithes as much as he could when he came to the parish'. Johnes refused separate adjudication, allowing the rector the full 20 per cent increase. His own rough calculation valued the tithes at £333 14s. 7½d. 'It would appear that the rent charge is low, but the award is for the full amount which the law allows'.[74]

Despite the wrangling, the commissioners' adjudication was usually accepted. The most vexatious part of the commutation process concerned apportionments. The verdict of the apportioner was regularly challenged. There were two main reasons for this. Apportioners were not the professionals in commutation proceedings that assistant commissioners were, and were in general more prone to error. Perhaps more important, however, was that many landowners did not properly understand the Commutation Act. They challenged decisions only when they saw how much rent charge had been placed on their own lands. It was often not appreciated that an apportionment appeal could succeed only if a proprietor showed that his lands were unfairly burdened in comparison with other lands in the tithe district. It was not competent to offer the vague objection that lands were 'highly rated'. Such an objection usually reflected nothing more than the fact that the rent charge had been increased generally.

John Bennett, an experienced tithe valuer, outlined his problems as a tithe apportioner in 1838:

> The difficulties of effecting agreements between the tithe owners and tithe payers, are as nothing in comparison with the difficulties of fairly and equitably apportioning the gross sum among the landowners, to the satisfaction of all. The landowners are mostly of one mind while they have the tithe owner to contend with; but when that question is disposed of, they begin to think of their individual interests and are opposed to each other as to the principle upon which the rent charge should be divided.
>
>   The man who has been occupying the estate in a manner to produce the greatest value of tithe, contends that he has too large a proportion of tillage to form the proper basis of adjustment for ever; and on the other hand the man who has been in the contrary extreme and has occupied his estate so as to yield the tithe owner very little, or perhaps nothing, contends that the apportionment should be made on the basis of the existing mode of occupation, and that because he has paid little or nothing for seven years, or for twenty years, or more, he cannot be charged with what he has not paid.[75]

Apportionment appeals were numerous and the following few examples must serve to indicate the most common grounds: at Muncaster (Cumberland), one proprietor, John Brown, argued that his 6¾-acre field had been saddled with too high a rent charge in view of the fact that it was 'grass and has not been ploughed for 100 years. It is subject to all tithes except Hay and Agistment'.[76] The valuer, William Dickinson, contended that

Brown's land was so much better than his neighbour's 'both as respects Tithable produce and productive quality that I am justified in putting at least 1s 0d. per acre more rent charge on former [*sic*] than on the latter'. With corroborative evidence from another local tithe valuer to support Dickinson, the assistant commissioner rejected the appeal. At Ambleton (Pembroke), W. C. A. Phillips objected that his lands were charged proportionately higher than those of his neighbours, and contended that, as he had not given his consent to the mode of apportionment being followed, he should not be bound by the decisions reached.[77] The tithe commissioners reaffirmed that the 'Act gives a certain portion of the landowners' power to make rules and we should not require them [the proprietors] to be unanimous'.

A very large number of appeals were in reality objections to the total rent charge awarded. In the parish of St. Michael, Lichfield, Assistant Commissioner George Cooke found the proprietors 'generally discontented with the rent charge and protesting that it was exorbitant'.[78] He had patiently to explain to them that any appeal against the total rent charge should have been made as a proper award appeal before the apportioner had been appointed. 'I had no power to enter into the question. Nothing was stated which led me to suppose that any error had occurred in the computations upon which the rent charge was founded, although the rent charge is undoubtedly a high equivalent of the tithe.' At Littleton (Hants.), A. O. Baker rapidly dismissed the only appeal against the apportionment on the grounds that 'it lay rather to the total amount of rent charge than to the sum charged upon his land'.[79]

Part of the trouble, however, lay with the incompetence of many valuers. Jelinger Symons expressed his distrust in 1839: 'I have seen too much of the local valuers of land to place much confidence in their decisions, and I would much sooner trust to the statements of the tenants themselves'.[80] The commissioners' report to Parliament in 1841 complained of frequent errors in drawing up tithe maps. Many of these were unconscious, but there was evidence that on some occasions maps and measurements had been deliberately fudged. Errors had been made which 'they attempt to conceal by tampering and making compensatory errors in the field books or original records of admeasurements'.[81]

In the early 1840s, particularly, apportioners and valuers were working under tremendous pressure. The early reports of the commissioners regretted the fact that a back-log of work had built up. Apportioners were expected to work quickly, and errors naturally crept in. Charles Howard had to direct many corrections to be made to the Darlaston (Staffs.) award after appeals in 1842, and numerous adjustments were made to the Gnosall apportionment in 1839.[82] There is no doubt that many incorrect apportionments slipped through the net. Samuel Bate commented on one such when, in November 1849, he wrote to the Duke of Sutherland's Staffordshire solicitor, Robert Fenton, about the commutation for the district of Beech in the parish of Stone. He had arranged some minor readjustments of rent charge. 'The award is very inaccurate. However, the award is made and confirmed and as the Church is not interested I presume the Commissioners will not care much about the accuracy or consistency of the award'.[83]

Rent charge settlements were not intended to favour tithe owners as much as enclosure arrangements had done. Enclosure settlements, effected usually during a period of boom, had taken into account the likely improved value of the land, and the tithe owner was able to insist on his share in improvements. The Commutation Act, by contrast, was passed at a time of considerable depression of corn prices. Tithe owners were not to share in any subsequent improvement of commuted land. As the Rev. C. A. Stevens commented: '... by the Commutation Act ... lands were absolutely discharged from the payment of all tithes ... The relations between the tithe-owner and the improved produce

(iv) Notice of Gross Tithe Rent Charge to be apportioned (from the Marton Tithe Award).

of the land were wholly destroyed. He was given, therefore, the dry value of a fixed number of bushels of corn in lieu of them. The *whole incremental value* of the tithes arising from increased produce was transferred absolutely to the landowner, and he has ever since drawn the whole profits of improvements by expenditure'.[84] Settlements at commutation were made on the basis of receipts rather than expectation. Nevertheless, the redefinition of rights enabled many owners to receive rather more after 1836 than they had done before. In Staffordshire, where it is possible to compare the pre-and post-commutation value of tithe and tithe rent charge in 151 tithe districts, 39.74 per cent of them showed rent charges within a £1 of the average values of 1829-35; 82 (54.3 per cent) showed increases, and only 5.69 per cent small decreases. Of the tithes thus increased in value, 15 were raised by more than 20 per cent. These large increases, which at first sight seem to conflict with cl.38 of the Commutation Act, were almost invariably the result of a decision by an assistant commissioner either that a modus was not supportable, or that a 'new' crop should be deemed tithable. At Draycott, for example, the rector's rent charge was raised from an average level of £339 to £423, largely because clover was considered tithable for the first time.[85] At Lyndhurst (Hants.), garden produce was deemed liable to tithe and the rector was awarded a rent charge £46 (22.54 per cent) in excess of his average receipts.[86] In the semi-industrial parish of Wednesbury (Staffs.), the vicar had received an average of £140 from his tithes, which included a modus in lieu of milk. The vicar successfully challenged this at commutation and his rent charge rose to £220 as a consequence.[87] At Gayton, the assistant commissioner declared various farm moduses invalid, and raised the rent charge to a level 24 per cent higher than the seven-year average.[88]

Such examples are exceptions, though by no means isolated ones. Large increases could only be permitted if the commissioners were convinced that the tithe owner had been disadvantaged by invalid claims for tithe exemption or if – as happened rarely – landowners voluntarily consented to give the tithe owner a large increase to his income. Perhaps more significant in the national picture was the systematic increase of rent charges by sums of up to 20 per cent. In the 1880s, when cereal prices were depressed by foreign competition, many tithe owners complained bitterly that commutation had been a thoroughly bad deal, yet in the short-term most had gained materially if never on the lavish scale seen at enclosure. They gained in two ways – by small but significant increases in their averages, and by receiving a clearly drawn irrefragable record of their rights. Many tithes uncertain of incidence, low in value and difficult to collect had been neglected before 1836. At Commutation, however, most of these had been added to the total value now invariably payable in cash on clear and unequivocal terms. Tithe owners gained more than is often realized in terms of sheer convenience.

A final benefit of Tithe Commutation was its cheapness. As has been seen, most of the formal costs of the tithe commission were met by the taxpayer. The only charges levied directly on the parties to commutation were solicitors' fees, and the costs of apportionment. The result was that, whereas enclosure costs had to be computed in pounds per acre, commutation costs were in shillings, and usually few shillings at that.[89] Assistant Commissioner George Lewis published the cost of commutation in the 2,600 acre parish of Budleigh (Devon) in 1845. The charges of valuer, surveyor, and solicitor, together with a few sundries, totalled £262 13s. 7d. or 2s. per acre.[90] At Yoxall, Staffordshire, where a straightforward voluntary agreement was concluded in 1838, the costs amounted to 1s. 4d. per acre. At neighbouring Hamstall Ridware, they totalled 2s. 4d.[91] Even at Lichfield, St. Chad, where there had been great difficulty in sorting out the ownership of tithes, and proceedings had dragged on for several years, they reached only 3s. 7d. and Assistant Commissioner George Cooke thought it necessary to add a defensive note to the commissioners: 'These expenses are heavy but they appear to be justified by the amount of work done. The Board is aware that the commutation has extended over many years and has been entangled with many most intricate questions at law'.[92]

Most of what costs there were fell on landowners rather than tithe owners. Landowners had to bear the entire cost of apportionment, and this was the lion's share. The tithe owner had to find only one half of the cost of ascertaining the proportion of waste, meadow, pasture and woodland in the district and one half of the solicitor's bill up to the time that a total rent charge was agreed or awarded. Thus, in the Yoxall instance referred to above, the tithe owner had to pay only £17 6s. 3d. of the total formal costs of £246.

Tithe Commutation was accomplished with remarkable smoothness and lack of rancour. Because the commissioners were prepared to trust the parties to know their own business, and because they were anxious to avoid uniform decisions which rode roughshod over local interests and knowledge, they aroused little hostility. An incompetent valuer or an officious assistant commissioner could be the source of much acrimony, but the bitterness remained essentially localized. Most parties eagerly seized the opportunity to put an end to the vagaries of the tithe system. Only in South Wales does there seem to have been any integrated regional hostility to commutation. There, corn prices had been much lower than the national average and the effect of working from a national rather than a local scale in ascertaining corn rents resulted in a large number of increases on average values. A study of Pembrokeshire tithe files indicates that the full 20 per cent increase authorized by cl.38 of the Tithe Act was regularly allowed by assistant commissioners. Many Welsh farmers were aggrieved, and tithe was one of the contributory factors in the Rebecca Riots of 1842-3.[93] A spokesman for the Welsh farmers admitted, however, that the commissioners were not acting improperly, as 'the provisions of the Tithe Act have been carried into execution with very great skill, judgement and accuracy'.[94]

Over the nation as a whole, the benefits of commutation greatly outweighed any minor disadvantages, Tithe was hopelessly anachronistic in an increasingly urban society. The Commutation Act sliced through its contradictions and complexities and made it possible for parties to effect a rational solution. No longer could a farmer's budget be upset by a new demand from the titheman or by an attack on an ancient customary payment; no longer would tithe owners have to grapple with fraud or guile by crafty, case-hardened proprietors determined to bully and cheat in order to pay as little as possible. After Commutation, for the first time the landowner knew clearly and in advance what he must pay, and the tithe owner what he might expect. The advantage was overwhelming.

SOURCE MATERIAL

Tithe maps were drawn up in triplicate, one copy for the tithe office, one for the parish clerk and one for the bishop of the diocese. The tithe office copies are now housed in the Public Office at Kew. The remaining copies are usually located in diocesan or county record offices, though some of the parochial copies still remain *in situ*. Maps were not drawn to any uniform scale. They varied from one to twelve chains to the inch, though most are on the three-, four-, or six-chains scales (26.6", 20" or 13" to the mile). Accompanying the map was a tithe apportionment; and many of the parochial and diocesan copies are still bound together with the map. The tithe apportionment consists of a preamble giving the extent and use of the acreage liable to tithe, the names of all tithe owners, and list all customary payments in lieu of tithe. The totals of rent charge awarded are given, and also the standard table for conversion to rent charge. The apportionment proper lists all landowners, tenants and fields in the tithe district. The land use of each field is usually defined as arable, meadow or pasture though some apportionments are more specific. Such a classification, of course, is of limited use to agricultural historians since it is not possible to infer, for example, when land is in long ley. The amount of rent charge apportioned on each field is given, and the totals are calculated for each landowner in a supplement at the end of the apportionment. Each field is given a reference number which relates to its position on the map.

The uses of such detailed material are obvious. The maps represent the first large-scale survey of the country ever produced and their information may be usefully compared with that provided by the 6' and 25' Ordnance Survey maps of the 1840s onwards. V. H. T. Skipp has stated that he would 'hesitate to tackle local research without the tithe award'. His Birmingham team began their parish histories by consulting the tithe map and award and compiling from them four separate maps: of landownership, of land occupation, of land utilization (arable, meadow or pasture), and of field-names. Given the tendency of many field names and not a few landowning families to remain the same over long periods of time, it is perfectly possible to use the tithe awards as a preliminary starting point even for a medieval study. Similarly, tithe awards may be used to identify particular properties mentioned in title deeds or other historical records. Evidence about field or estate boundaries, the latter readily identifiable by comparing map and apportionment, may be set against later evidence – the 1873 'New Domesday' survey, for example – to plot changes in the more recent period. Some maps may also be used to plot industrial developments, early railway lines and even suburban sprawl.[95]

The eager local historian must not be seduced into thinking, however, that maps and awards can provide reliable answers to all kinds of questions about mid-nineteenth century economic and social structure. The two major snares are inaccuracy and incompleteness. The surveys do not cover the entire country, since lands previously exonerated from tithe by enclosure or for any other reason are not usually surveyed. About 79 per cent of the area of England and Wales is covered by tithe maps. The most worrying problem is that a very large number of maps and apportionments are either incomplete or imperfect. The commissioners themselves were well aware that the maps were often rough approximations, as the evidence of their assistants, cited above,[96] indicates. In most cases the evidence of both map and apportionment as to size of tithe deposit, land use, names and extent of holdings of landowners and tenants should be regarded as at best a general guide rather than a definite statement.

The original concept intended something a good deal better. The commissioners had been charged by the Commutation Act with the responsibility of confirming a map and award for each tithe district once apportionment was complete. The commissioners saw merit in a proposal by Assistant Commissioner Dawson in late 1836 to use the opportunity to make a general or cadastral survey of the entire country, which could then be used for various purposes, including tax assessments and the operation of a Register of Real Property.[97] However, the commissioners' request for a general survey was rejected. It was argued that those who took advantage of the voluntary provisions of the Tithe Act could make use of existing surveys to avoid unnecessary expense in commissioning a new one. Commissioners were authorized to accept surveys known to be inaccurate if the parties concerned did not object. The cost of the commissioners' proposal for a first-class survey – estimated at £1,500,000 – was regarded in Parliament as an unacceptable additional burden on the landed interest. The compromise, to which the commissioners gave reluctant assent, was in amending legislation in 1837 and 1839.[98] Commissioners were able to confirm both voluntary and compulsory commutations even though they were not satisfied with the accuracy of the maps which accompanied them. They acknowledged two classes of award. Their seal was affixed to the first class, in which they declared themselves satisfied with the reliability of a purpose-designed map. Such an award could be subsequently cited as a true legal record. The second class, in which old surveys formed the basis of tithe maps, remained unsealed by the commissioners and could not be used as evidence of tenure and rights in a court of law. Thus, a very large number of inaccurate maps were submitted in order to save expense. It has been estimated that only one-sixth of all maps deposited with the commissioners (about 1,900) were deemed first class.[99] The records of the tithe commission are seriously flawed as a consequence. The commissioners themselves noted in 1841: 'Unquestionably we believe that the maps to which we have attached our Seal are very much more accurate than they would have been had they not gone through the ordeal of this Office ...'.[100]

Inaccuracy in unsealed maps is often detected by comparing them with evidence from estate papers. Mistakes are particularly prevalent on areas of tithe-free land within a tithe district; proprietors were naturally unwilling to pay for accurate mapping from which neither they nor the tithe owner could conceivably derive benefit. Frequently, older plans of varying accuracy were incorporated in the tithe map. Errors of transcription have also been discovered such that information on size or ownership differs between the tithe commissioners' copy and the diocesan or parish copy. Nor should it be forgotten that there was frequently a delay of four or five years between the making of a map and the final agreement to an apportionment. In such cases there may be significant discrepancies between the two on landownership and tenancy. In short, local historians should never rely on the information provided by the tithe map alone.

The tithe files in the Public Record Office are for the most part the working papers of the assistant commissioners. They show, sometimes in great detail, how decisions on rent charge were reached, and frequently include correspondence from assistant commissioners to the tithe office and what amount to minutes of award and apportionment appeal meetings. In addition, when a commutation was voluntary, assistant commissioners had to file a report on the fairness or otherwise of the agreement made. This included information on farming methods, soil fertility, and levels of rent. The material is thus of considerable interest to agricultural historians.[101] The files were drastically weeded in the early years of the twentieth century, and it seems that only those papers considered of direct relevance to the achievement of commutation were retained. Thus most correspondence between proprietors, tithe owners and assistant commissioners seems to have been excised, but what remains is of great interest and still relatively little used.

The 1836 Commutation Act was not the last word on tithes. New Acts had to be devised, notably in 1891, 1925 and 1936, to deal with changed circumstances.[102] Rent charge finally disappeared after 1936 with landowners paying an annuity over 60 years which would finally redeem all tithe by 1996. Most land has already been exonerated from payment as lump sums have been accepted in exoneration of outstanding burdens. Tithe is now little more than a folk memory, though many retain vivid memories of the 'tithe war' which precede the 1936 Act.[103] Just before Commutation, it was a burning issue on which the very future of the Church of England as an established body could be said to turn. The Commutation Act was one of the great reforming enactments of the 1830s and its place in settling one of the major sources of dispute in rural England and Wales deserves wider understanding and recognition.

NOTES

(Place of publication given when other than London.)

1. Most general textbooks mention the Act only in passing, if at all. See, for example, E. L. Woodward, *The Age of Reform, 1851-70* (2nd ed., 1962) and R. K. Webb, *Modern England* (1969), pp.227-8 and 610-11. J. F. C. Harrison, *The Early Victorians, 1832-1851* (1971) ignores it. Even modern specialist agricultural studies play down its importance. F. M. L. Thompson, *English Landed Society in the Nineteenth Century* (1963) and E. L. Jones, *The Development of English Agriculture, 1815-73* (1968) ignore it. There is a brief reference in J. D. Chambers and G. E. Mingay, *The Agricultural Revolution, 1750-1880* (1966), p.149. Only Lord Ernle, over seventy years ago, thought tithes worthy of a chapter and the Commutation Act worth explanation, *English Farming Past and Present* (6th ed., 1961), pp.332-48.
2. *Quarterly Review*, lvii (1836), pp.242-3.
3. For amplification on this point, see Eric J. Evans, 'Tithing Customs and Disputes: The evidence of Glebe Terriers', *Agric. Hist. Rev.* xviii (1970), pp.17-35. For the problems of tithing in kind, see Eric J. Evans, *The Contentious Tithe* (1976), pp.21-26.
4. See, for example, the valuation of tithes at Midridge (Durham), Durham, D/EL Box 23. William Marshall gives impressionistic calculations in *Rural Economy of the Midland Counties*, 2 vols. (2nd ed., 1796), i, 17, and Arthur Young in *A General View of the Agriculture of the County of Hertfordshire* (1804), pp.30-31.
5. Staffs., R.O., D.593/G/3/4/2-67.
6. Lancs., R.O. DD Gr. (uncatalogued), Thirkens to Greene, 19 May 1828.
7. O. F. Christie (ed.) *The Diary of Rev. William Jones*, 1777-1821 (1929), p.147.
8. See, for example, the work of John Mee Matthew in Staffordshire, Public Record Office, IR 18/9357 and 9377, and John Johnes in Pembroke, IR/14603, 14604.
9. Ernle, *op. cit.,* p.341. Chambers and Mingay endorse the view, *op. cit.,* p.46.
10. F. M. Eden, *The State of the Poor*, 3 vols. (1797). The replies to the enquiry presented to Pitt are filed in P.R.O. 30/8/310, pp.1-12.
11. The rules for the establishment of a valid modus are set out in F. Plowden, *The Principles and Law of Tithing* (1806), pp.198-207. These are discussed in E. J. Evans, 'A History of the Tithe System in England, 1690-1850, with special reference to Staffordshire'. (University of Warwick, Ph.D. thesis, 1970), pp.86-93.
12. Anon., *Observation on a General Commutation of Tithes for Land for a Corn Rent* (1782), p.5.
13. *Annals of Agriculture*, xix (1793), p.67.
14. *British Magazine*, i (1832), p.387.
15. Eric J. Evans, 'A Nineteenth Century Tithe Dispute and its Significance: The Case of Kendal', *Trans. Cumberland and Westmorland Antiqu. & Archaeol. Soc.* lxxiv (1974), pp.159-183.
16. Eric J. Evans, *The Contentious Tithe*, pp.50-58.
17. Lichfield Joint Record Office, B/V/6, Haughton, 1766.
18. Over 60 per cent of the 3,700 or so Enclosure Acts passed between 1757 and 1835 eliminated tithe payments. Landowners were prepared to pay handsomely to be rid of the burden of tithes. Many Acts passed during the boom years of the 1790s allowed tithe owners as much as one quarter of the arable land in compensation, and one – Shipton (Hants.) – gave the tithe owner 30 per cent. (W. R. Ward, 'The Tithe Question in England in the Early Nineteenth Century', *Jnl. Ecc. Hist.* xvii (1965), p.70). During the boom years, in fact, the most usual stated settlement was one fifth of the arable land and one eighth or one ninth of the usually less profitable meadow or pasture land. Later enclosure settlements were rather less favourable to tithe owners, particularly when arable farmers experienced hardship after 1815. The predominant feeling was that settlements during the years of plenty had been too generous, and many later settlements turned to cash payments in the form of corn rents, in preference to extending the freehold interests of the Church and lay impropriators. Enclosure provided a useful testing ground for solutions to the tithe problem and enabled reformers to cite precedents for their proposals. Without it, the road to commutation would have been stonier and its implementation hampered by far more pitfalls.

19. 6 & 7 Wil.IV, cap.77., 1 & 2 Vict., cap.106, and 3 & 4 Vict., cap.113.

20. For more detail see W. L. Mathieson, *English Church Reform, 1815-1840* (1923), and O. Brose, *Church and Parliament, 1828-1860* (Stanford, 1959), pp.136-56.

21. Adam Smith, *The Wealth of Nations* (2 vols., Everyman Edn. 1910), i,p.347.

22. *Ibid.*, i,pp.318-19.

23. *Farmers' Magazine*, iv (1803), p.65.

24. W. Corbett, *Political Register*, xiii (1808), p.250. For other examples see *Farmers' Magazine*, x (1810), pp.466-8, and J. Middleton, *A General View of the Agriculture of the County of Middlesex* (1795), p.59.

25. Richard Jones, *Remarks on the Government Bill for the Commutation of Tithe* (3rd. ed. 1837), p.5.

26. Morgan Cove, *An Essay on the Revenues of the Church of England*, (2nd. ed. 1797), p.252.

27. The present writer has taken issue with the current orthodoxy of agrarian historians on this point. Eric J. Evans, *The Contentious Tithe*, pp.72-76.

28. *The Times*, 17 April 1834.

29. See his speech in Parliament, Hansard, 1st ser. xxxiv (1816), cols.365-9 and 685-704. There is a very uncritical portrait of Curwen in Henry Lonsdale, *The Worthies of Cumberland* (1867), pp.3-204.

30. *House of Commons Journals*, lxxi (1816), p.391.

31. HCJ. lxxiii (1818), p.140. The debate may be found in Hansard, 1st ser. xxxvi (1817), cols.1070-6.

32. 6 Geo. IV, cap.28 and 6 Geo. IV cap.22.

33. The Bill is found in HCJ lxxxii (1828), pp.282-320. Peel's speech is in Hansard, 2nd ser xviii (1828), cols.1151-61.

34. E. J. Hobsbawm and G. F. E. Rudé, *Captain Swing* (1969), esp. Appendix iii, pp.312-59.

35. See, for example, petitions from Rochester, HCJ, lxxv (1830), 18 May; Frensbury, *ibid.*, 8 February; Holt (Norfolk), *ibid.*, 5 March; and Llanthewy, *ibid.*, 12 March.

36. Hansard, 2nd ser., xxiv (1830), col.819.

37. Henry Ryder, *Charge to the Clergy of the Diocese of Lichfield and Coventry* (1832), pp.12-14. William Salt Library, Stafford. Collection of Visitation Charges.

38. The fullest account of these activities is Michael Brock, *The Great Reform Act* (1973), pp.231-67.

39. 2 & 3. Wil. IV, cap.100.

40. 4 & 5. Wil. IV, cap.83.

41. 5 & 6. Wil. IV, cap.74.

42. House of Commons Journals, lxxxix (1834), 18 April.

43. For the debate on the 1834 Bill, see Hansard, 3rd ser., xxii (1834), cols.818-42.

44. Howley to Russell, 31 December 1834. Lambeth Palace Library, MS 1812, ff.3-4.

45. Quoted in H. J. Hanham, *The Nineteenth Century Constitution* (Cambridge, 1969), p.215.

46. For the debate in March 1835 see Hansard, 3rd ser., xxvii (1835), cols.170-202.

47. Hansard, 3rd ser., xxi (1838), col.185.

48. The original Bill is in Parl. Papers (HC), 1836, iv, pp.125 ff. It contained 54 clauses to the Act's 97.

49. *The Times*, 11 February 1836.

50. Hansard, 3rd ser., xxxiii (1836), col.505.

51. *Ibid.*, col.721.

52. 6 & 7 Wil. IV, cap.71.

53. Hansard, 3rd ser. xxxii (1836), cols.607-15 and 1619-24.

54. *DNB*, x, 1045.

55. Buckinghamshire R.O., D.85/33. Jones to Townsend, 1 July 1837.

56. Parl. Papers, (HC) 1844, v, cl.23.

57. 1 & 2 Vict., cap.64.

58. 2 & 3 Vict., cap.62.

59. 9 & 10 Vict., cap.73.

60. Arthur Taylor's pamphlet *Laissez Faire and State Intervention in Nineteenth-Century Britain* (1972) does not mention it. The specialist studies cited in his admirable bibliography at best accord it a brief reference. The present author willingly acknowledges his vested interest in furthering knowledge of the tithe commission, but reasserts that its role is important and imperfectly understood.

61. Calculations from Yearly Reports of the Tithe Commission to Parliament. Parl. Papers (HC) 1837-52, *passim.*

62. Parl. Papers (HC), 1851, xxii, p.549.

63. P.R.O. IR 18/9418.

64. *Ibid.* 4111.

65. Parl. Papers (HC) 1837-8, xxviii, pp.33-36.
66. P.R.O. IR 18/716.
67. *Ibid.* 18/3560.
68. *Ibid.* 9059.
69. *Ibid.* 9545.
70. *Ibid.* 9258.
71. *Ibid.* 9346. IR 29/32/88. See also the letter from the Tithe Commission in Staffs. R.O. D.1851/4/7.
72. Copies are regularly found among estate and solicitors' papers. See, for example, Staffs. R.O. D.240/M/D/vii/3.
73. P.R.O. IR 18/14602.
74. *Ibid.* 14606.
75. J. B. H. Bennett, *Letters and Observations on the Subject of Tithe Apportionment* (1839), p.5.
76. P.R.O. IR 18/710.
77. *Ibid.* 14602.
78. *Ibid.* 9422.
79. *Ibid.* 9056.
80. Report on a voluntary agreement at Bobbington (Staffs.), *ibid.* 9268.
81. Parl. Papers (HC) 1841, xii, pp.141-4.
82. P.R.O. IR 18/9333 and 9370.
83. Staffs. R.O. D.593/T/10/11.
84. C. A. Stevens, *Land-Rental, Tithes and Tithe-Surcharge* (1887), p.21.
85. P.R.O. IR 18/9335.
86. *Ibid.* 9061.
87. *Ibid.* 9536.
88. *Ibid.* 9369.
89. Recent research suggests that historians have under-estimated the expense of enclosure. See two Retailed county surveys, J. M. Martin, 'The Cost of Parliamentary Enclosure in Warwickshire', *Univ. Birmingham Hist. Jnl.*, ix (1964), pp.146-56, and M. E. Turner, 'The Cost of Parliamentary Enclosure in Buckinghamshire', *Agric. Hist. Rev.* xxi (1973), pp.35-46.
90. P.R.O. IR 18/1170.
91. Staffs. R.O. D.1851/4/12.
92. P.R.O. IR 18/9303.
93. For which see D. Williams, *The Rebecca Riots* (Cardiff, 1955), pp.55, 129-36, 234-5 and 239.
94. Letter in *The Times*, 11 October 1843.
95. V. H. T. Skipp, 'The Place of Team Work in Local History' in H. P. R. Finberg and V. H. T. Skipp (eds.) *Local History, Objective and Pursuit* (Newton Abbot, 1967), pp.87-102, see esp. pp.94-5. On the use of tithe material in general, see L. M. Munby, 'Tithe Apportionments and Maps', *History*, liv (1969), pp.68-71 and J. B. Harley, 'Maps for the Local Historian: 3, Enclosure and Tithe Maps', *Amateur Historian*, vii (1966-7), pp.265-74.
96. See above pp.26-7.
97. F. M. L. Thompson, *Chartered Surveyors: The Growth of a Profession* (1968), pp.104-6.
98. 1 Vict. cap. 69 and 2 & 3 Vict. cap. 62, cl.22. The 1839 Act extended the Commissioners' power to confirm inaccurate maps which accompanied compulsory awards.
99. H. C. Prince, 'The Tithe Surveys of the Mid-Nineteenth Century', *Agric. Hist. Rev.* vii (1959), p.23.
100. Parl. Papers (HC) 1841, xii, pp.141-4.
101. On the tithe files, see E. A. Cox and B. R. Dittimer, 'The Tithe Files of the Mid-Nineteenth Century', *Agric. Hist. Rev.* xiii (1965), pp.1-16. For a survey of materials for the study of changing patterns of landownership in the mid-nineteenth century, see the computer-aided study of Kentish tithe awards in R. J. P. Kain, 'Tithe Surveys and Landownership', *Jnl. Hist. Geog.* i (1975), pp.39-48. R. J. P. Kain, 'The Tithe Commutation Surveys', *Archaeologia Cantiana*, vol. lxxxix, pp.101-18 (1974), and 'B. K. Dawson's Proposal in 1836 for a Cadastral Survey of England and Wales', *Journal of the British Cartographic Society*, December 1975, pp.81-8.
102. The story of tithe after 1850 is briefly sketched in Eric J. Evans, *The Contentious Tithe*, pp.163-68.
103. Doreen Wallace, *The Tithe War* (1934) presents a partisan account. The tithe war was also the subject of a BBC2 television programme in the 'Yesterday's Witness' series. It was screened on 25 May 1972 and 11 August 1973.

TRANSCRIPT

Preamble to a Voluntary Agreement to Commute Tithes

Whereas an Agreement for the Commutation of Tithes in the Township of Marton in the Parish of Poulton in the County of Lancaster was, on the eighth day of February in the Year One Thousand Eight Hundred and Thirty nine, confirmed by the Tithe Commissioners for England and Wales, of which Agreement, with the Schedule therein comprised, the following is a Copy: A Provisional Agreement for the Commutation of the Tithes of the Township of Marton in the Parish of Poulton in the County of Lancaster pursuant to the Act for the Commutation of Tithes in England and Wales made and executed at a Meeting duly called and holden within the said Township and adjourned from time to time and holden by adjournment on the thirtieth day of November in the year one thousand eight hundred and thirty eight and since perfected by and between Henry Bence Bence of Thorington Hall in the County of Suffolk Esquire and Edmund Ker Cranstoun Bacon of Wilton Place Knightsbridge in the County of Middlesex Esquire Impropriators and Owners in equal moieties of all the Great Tithes of the said Township (other than and except the Tithe of Hay) of the first part the Reverend John Hull Vicar of the said Parish of Poulton and as such Vicar Owner of the Tithe of Hay and all the small Tithes of the said Township of the second part John Fairclough Clerk of the Parish Church of Poulton aforesaid and as such Clerk entitled to receive a certain Modus or Ancient customary yearly payment of Five shillings and sixpence in respect of the Vacarial Tithes of certain Lands within the said Township as hereinafter mentioned of the third part and the several persons Owners of Land within the said Township by whom or by whose Agents duly authorised in that behalf these presents are executed and the interest of which Land Owners of the said Township is not less than two thirds of the Land therein subject to Tithes of the fourth part —

The Township of Marton aforesaid contains by estimation Four thousand four hundred and five acres two roods and twenty-seven perches of Land Statute Measure.

The quantity in Statute Measure of Lands within the said Township which is now cultivated as Arable Meadow and Pasture Land or otherwise is as follows namely —

	a.	r.	p.
Arable	1,639	2	10
Meadow	627	2	20
Pasture Land with Homesteads Gardens Sites and Wastes	2,138	1	37
	4,405	2	27